Life Happens

Also by Cynthia Hallam and published by Ginninderra Press
Bread and Butter People
Rising to the Occasion
Town Life
Living in the Moment
Moving with the Times
New Horizons
Here and Now

Cynthia Hallam

Life Happens

Acknowledgements

With enduring thanks to my daughter Trish for her unfailing support and fearless editing. Warren Nicholls and Roz Vrielink for keeping our writing group on their toes and Stephen Matthews for his ongoing faith in my efforts.

Dedication

For Trish and Peter,
Michael and Ben
with love

Life Happens
ISBN 978 1 76109 073 8
Copyright © text Cynthia Hallam 2021
Cover photo © Ginninderra Press

First published 2021 by
Ginninderra Press
PO Box 3461 Port Adelaide 5015 Australia
www.ginninderrapress.com.au

Contents

Going Forward	7
Rivals	8
Choices	9
In the Eyes of the Beholders	10
Precautions	11
Impasse	12
Trust	13
Rain	14
Conjecture	15
Misadventure	16
Bookworms	17
Thunderstruck!	18
A Lucky Country	19
Switching Off	20
Out of the Blue	21
A Bit of a Mystery	22
The Paradox	23
It's That Time Again	24
Another New Beginning	25
Kids!	26
A New Perspective	27
Intuition	28
Unexpected Delight	29
Jubilation	30
Crosswords	31
Petty Irritations	32
A New Temptation	33
An Idle Speculation	34
Simple Pleasures	35
Decluttering	36

Choice	37
Partners	38
The Good Life	39
Shopping	40
Shifting Sands	41
Recognition	42
Possibilities?	43
Innocence	44
Jumping the Gun	45
Mothercraft	46
Misnomer	47
A Fresh Outlook	48
Gratification	49
Brainwaves	50
A Fruitful Thought	51
Feline Routine	52
Azaleas	53
A Symptom of the Times	54
Manoeuvres	55
Just Raising a Point	56

Going Forward

The passage of time is unavoidable
and whether we are ready or not,
marches us inexorably into the future,
and sometimes, I can't help wonder
what the odyssey might have in store.

Will the superpowers be content
with what they may already possess
and not cross swords with each other?
Any climate changes evolve gently
and are confined to the sustainable?
Will people value people again
instead of cosying up to the internet?

While our wishes for a Utopian world
can remain just a fanciful dream,
it would seem that the best we can do
is generate a vibrant personal history
and with hope springing eternal,
make our own lives worth the journey.

Rivals

The kookaburras and magpies
are in full voice this morning,
an unseasonal, cooling breeze
encouraging rejoicing
for this very welcome respite
from summer's relentless heat.

As I seize the opportunity
to tackle a backlog of weeds,
the choristers are waiting
in the trees nearby
to claim the insects and worms
dislodged by my endeavours.

Inside for a cuppa and a rest,
I watch the magpies,
who were quicker off the mark,
scratching and pouncing,
warbling their delight
while the mute kookaburras
contemplate the option
of dining somewhere else
and swoop away to investigate.

Choices

She is young and remarkably pretty,
a tangle of auburn hair falling to her shoulders
with artless abandon,
her brief shorts and top emphasising
the attractiveness of her blossoming figure.

But such a shame her arms have been defaced
by all those tattoos
which to me, lack any hint of competent artistry,
and I can barely contain my disappointment
at such wilful desecration.

Then angst turns to pity, for as she moves on
I notice an eye-catching, heart-enclosed 'Ryan'
and can only hope
that in light of this youthful, trusting naivety,
he genuinely intends to stay in her life forever.

In the Eyes of the Beholders

Florence can only be described as a real goer.
Well past her 80th birthday
she mows her lawn, plays competition bowls,
and can change a light bulb in a flash.
She organises the regular Red Cross stalls
and is an enthusiastic volunteer
at the nursing home around the corner.

She has just started painting her house
even though concerned neighbours advised
that because of her advancing years
she should be getting someone in,
but she informed them in no uncertain terms
that she is not THAT old,
sees ageing as having been younger longer
and assuring them that she is
well down the queue at the pearly gates
and in absolutely no danger
of being upgraded, thank you very much!

Precautions

It is high summer,
that time of the year
when the senses
of mountain dwellers
sharpen
and sometimes,
a quick sniff outside
in the morning
and before bed
can become routine,
noses on alert
for any hint
of bushfire smoke
in our vicinity.

A positive whiff
prompts reminders
of prearranged plans
and location
of family and friends
but if reassured
by no siren's wail,
trust that
further away,
the situation
is under control,
but will still top up
the fuel in the car
just in case.

Impasse

The wisteria's off again.
Seemingly overnight,
it has bullied shrubs,
engulfed plants
and snaked up trees,
clinging on with
a boa constrictor's grip
that no tugging
can release
until a satisfying snip
leaves it withering
and releasing its hold.

None of the digging
to find its primary root
ever yields
any positive results
so wisteria clones
keep appearing
until autumn weather
chills them to a halt,
but aware that
despite the hiatus,
our battle
is in no way over yet!

Trust

The rescue dog living down the road
seems to be responding
to the love and care of his new family.
When our paths first crossed
during my regular evening walks,
he was obviously, very much on edge,
distrust of strangers mirrored in his eyes
as he rejected my friendly overtures.

But these days, he is more responsive
to my outstretched hand
and encouraged by his owner's smile,
gives a cautious sniff then backs away,
uncertain of my actual intent,
a defence mechanism still on automatic.

The ribs of the huge Great Dane cross
are much less prominent now
and I have real hopes that before long,
he will greet me with a wagging tail,
accept a gentle fondle of his ears
with little to fear and a growing trust
that not all humans are the same
as those he had previously encountered.

Rain

Ending a dry, sunburnt, country summer,
the heaviest downpour of the season
is more than welcome.
In shock, the grass, barely clinging to life,
is taking its time
to absorb this long-awaited salvation,
roots in the baked-hard soil
briefly resisting the timely reprieve,
but listless shrubs are already perking up,
tanks are refilling, dust laid to rest,
heat a bit more bearable,
and while the media is reporting
dislocated traffic and blown-out umbrellas
only the city dwellers on the coast
are not smiling.

Conjecture

The worst house in the street
must be having some work done at last.
A removalist's van is pulling away,
contractor's ute parked outside
and a Portaloo already being installed
by the latticed front veranda.

Will the renovations stretch to
the rusting roof, drooping guttering
and flaking weatherboards?
Even the front fence needs an overhaul
before the letter box, with a last gasp,
finally tumbles onto the verge.

The builder is just leaving,
waved off by someone I do not know.
Is the old owner in a nursing home
and an inheritor moving in?
A speculator tarting up an investment?
Knock down/rebuild possible?

I resist the urge to enquire,
but like the rest of us in the vicinity,
will keep a very close eye
on the progress of the resurrection
in case our place may then be judged
the worst house in the street.

Misadventure

A neighbouring cat has come visiting.
At first I thought it was a stray
but now recognise it as one I had seen
sunning itself on a nearby veranda.
I watch its leisurely progress
as it is sniffing around the backyard
satisfying its natural curiosity
before springing onto a gumtree stump,
home to an oversize, ceramic mouse
then bewildered, hastily retreats.

An avian tourist lands on the birdbath
for some opportunistic refreshment
and rump bristling in excitement,
the wily feline is measuring its leap
as I scramble to the bird's defence,
but a resident magpie swoops down
to chase the usurping drinker off
and amid the chaos, the tabby bolts,
further exploration of this alien terrain
possibly postponed indefinitely.

Bookworms

Despite all the forecasts by the electronic media,
I hope that printed fiction won't disappear.
Propped up in bed or relaxing in a chair
we can escape for a while our own daily reality.
Intriguing situations and relationships in the past,
present or a future century can be explored,
swept along by an author's innovative imagination,
holding the volume of words a solid connection.

There'll be some that won't retain our interest
despite an appealing cover and praise on the back,
but although it is always only make-believe,
books entertain, engage the lonely, pass the time,
build an ongoing relationship with the story
that a fleeting, illuminated screen can't emulate.
But here I am ranting when my trusty bookmark
is waiting for my totally unbiased attention.

Thunderstruck!

After an extended summer and brief autumn,
the early, icy blast has caught us all by surprise.
Trees, barely into accommodating the annual fall
are still half clothed.
Birds, totally misled by the unseasonal warmth
have delayed their migration north too long
and huddle against the wind in sparse canopies.

Blankets and coats are being hastily retrieved
from summer storage,
the usual preparations for the winter months
distracted by the ongoing salubrious days,
but reminded now, by the frosty turnaround,
that regardless of science's evolution,
Mother Nature is still in control of our weather.

A Lucky Country

The local newspaper has just arrived.
Residents complain of highway congestion,
Council priorities are being questioned
and asbestos removal is of major concern.
A reduction of waste to landfill is vital
and a junior soccer team unlucky to lose.

Overseas, students may be shooting others,
families are being gassed by chemicals,
millions are now homeless due to civil wars
and floods wiping out entire villages
but look at this! I have only just noticed!
Someone's Labradoodle has gone missing!

Switching Off

In an increasingly digitalised environment,
now and then it can be beneficial to escape
into a therapeutic world of natural reality.

In the bush, a bellbird's trilling could be
the tuning fork for a soothing, avian choir.
Rustling leaf whispering can calm the stress
of keeping on top of the latest technology,
the earthy, undergrowth aroma relaxing,
powering down the grip of any anxiety.

At the beach, the ozone will infuse feelings
of a welcome holiday for all the senses,
prompt overdue reviews of our blessings.
The sand massaging our feet eases tension
while watching dolphins play, seagulls soar.
Hear the rhythmic to and fro of the surf.

In the park, just resting on a shaded bench
or strolling along a jasmine-scented path
can promote an unexpected tranquillity,
away for just a while, from the temptation
of dangerously addictive gaming screens
or compulsion to bare our lives to others.

So perhaps nature has always understood
what innovators may soon need to learn.
That the average mind has a finite capacity.

Out of the Blue

Nothing is as uplifting as the kindness of strangers.
Like that supporting hand preventing my fall,
the young girl on the bus, observing my concern,
confirming that we are heading for the station
and googling the time of my connection.
The theatre goer in the foyer tapping my shoulder
with the ticket unknowingly dropped.
The shared umbrella over a pedestrian crossing
when caught in an unforeseen, passing shower
and hope that as the tapestry of my life unfolds,
the circumstances may arise to pass on to others
a timely gift of unexpected compassion.

A Bit of a Mystery

Why do usually smart people do silly things
like using such ridiculous endearments
for those they really care about?
Honestly, Pumpkin, Honeybun and Baby Doll.
Tiddlywinks, Snookums, or something like
Mugwump, Bozo, Cleverdick or Muscles.
And what about our poor defenceless pets.
Can you believe Mum's Itty Bitty Woof Woof?
Fluffwuffy, Slobberchops or Tweetypie?
I mean, it is all rather demeaning isn't it,
so I trust that my own dear little feline Tess
totally understands the well known fact
that Toodlypoops is another word for love.

The Paradox

Following a week of grey, cloudy skies,
today is full of light and shade
after the desperately needed rain
has ceased at last.
The garden is bursting with new life,
drooping plants standing to attention
in homage to their saviour.
The pinks and lavender of the azaleas
and jacarandas are enticing the eye.
Patches of grass in the shadows
of spring's fresh canopy of leaves
already appear to be a little greener.
Even the birds seem more enthusiastic.

Our daily routine is picking up again
to its usual momentum
after being plagued by the blues
as the constant showers got us down
in spite of our relief and delight
at the easing of the drought
and bathed once more in sunshine
our days are regaining purpose,
the lift in spirits carrying us on
until the next welcome wet weather
has us applauding nature's bounty
and hopefully, not be a precursor
to the illogical grumps of cabin fever.

It's That Time Again

With December still in its infancy,
Christmas festivities are well under way.
Antlers are now sprouting on cars,
staff parties being organised.
Shops are awash with all the trappings
and the rotation of carols and songs
ramping up towards saturation.

As we celebrate the reason for it all,
indulgent conviviality will continue
until New Year's Eve brings a timely halt
with its usual rueful resolutions
but as always, come next December,
we'll be more than ready to embrace
whatever the season has to offer.

Another New Beginning

New Year's morning and the street is resting peacefully,
everyone still sleeping in or nursing their recovery
after last night's conclusion to the hectic, festive season.
Just one man and his golden retriever are passing by
as I force my feet to get moving on my regular walk
before the expected swelter begins sapping my energy.

High in the trees, the annual cicada liberation choir
doesn't seem as strident as usual, just full of hope
as I ponder what the year to come might have in store,
sip a cool drink back beneath the comfort of the fan
and decide it is all too deep to think about now.
That, in fact, I would be much better off just winging it.

Kids!

Now as big as herself,
Mother magpie's child
follows in her wake,
beak wide open,
squawking demands
to assuage its hunger.
But with no luck today,
it lies on its back
and throws a tantrum,
like a toddler in a shop
denied a wanted lolly
but Mum struts on
to settle behind a bush
as if embarrassed by
the performance.

But the rebellious rant
has achieved nothing,
so the gyrations cease,
and feathers askew,
the recalcitrant
starts pecking at grass
in the approved way
until Mother returns,
deposits at its feet
a wriggling reward
then swiftly moves on
as maternal patience
is finally justified.

A New Perspective

He finally decided it was time to give up driving
when his ancient Holden gave up the ghost.
Anyway, it would be safer travelling on a bus
because these days, as far as he was concerned,
there were too many idiots hooning on the roads,
blind drunk, stoned or being plain stupid,
and those who were using a new fangled phone
were not even looking at the road, were they?

But he started worrying that some of the drivers
were too inexperienced to cope with problems
that may suddenly arise along the route
and decided that from now on, he would walk,
which to be quite honest, was not much fun
when it was too hot or the rain was pelting down
but at least he was still in control of his own life
and never at the mercy of incompetent strangers.

But then, he tripped over his stick and wound up
with a broken leg in the emergency ward
where the doctors and nurses looked too young
to have his welfare in their hands but seemed
to actually know what they were doing.
Accepted that, for a while at least, he no longer
had a say in the way that he preferred to live
but may be quite nice not having to cook dinner.

Intuition

Nuzzles on my cheek and loud vibrating purrs
wake me to the fact that her breakfast time
is probably well and truly overdue.
My elderly feline Tess is a stickler for routine
but a sleep-in would have been welcome
and I can't help wondering if all indoor cats
have some built in antenna
for her understanding of my daily habits
is truly amazing.

When the jug goes on during busy mornings,
she knows my lap will soon be available
and is ready and waiting to take possession
before I've had the chance to enjoy a sip.
Lift a book or remote and there she is,
prodding her brush to the floor
to capture my otherwise engaged attention
if her usual grooming has been delayed
which is annoying.

But generally, if I give it some thought,
some manoeuvring by my furry companion
is a tendency I am willing to tolerate.
Most of the time!

Unexpected Delight

In the breakfast food aisle,
her smile is genuinely warm
and can't help responding,
wondering who it is
I must have forgotten,
but noting my bemusement
she pats my arm,
'Don't worry,' she says.
'Just passing on the smile
I received a while ago,
and made me feel so good,
had the need to share it.'

While together, each of us
ponders our selections,
my own relieved smile
is answered by another
and in the register queue,
find myself transferring it
to someone else
with such sheer pleasure
that the rest of my day
has been quite revitalised
by the unforeseen,
rewarding experience.

Jubilation

It seems that the only vacant shop in town
has been leased at last.
The news is blazoned victoriously
over the newspaper lining the front window
and I can't help wondering
just who might be giving it a go.
What business could make a success of it.

Retail wise we are already being catered for
and the coffee shops and takeaways
have been serving us well
but I guess there will always be room
for a new opportunity,
something to excite, make our wallets itch
and hope their faith will be rewarded.

Crosswords

She finally had to admit to herself
that her current addiction
was seriously interfering with her life.
Housework was now a hurried affair,
cooking a swift, last minute necessity.
Library books were always overdue
and her regular exercise routine
had become only a distant memory.

At first just a pleasant diversion,
it soon claimed most of her attention,
for like a Christmas Secret Santa,
you never knew what you would get.
They either almost solved themselves
or she was absolutely stumped
from the very first enigmatic clue.
(What's a 'large ungulate' anyway?)

So she decided that once and for all
she would distance herself
from the seductive crossword books
bringing her current life undone,
but certain that it would not matter
if she quickly tackled one more,
she opened up her wordy nemesis
and contemplated 'Has self-control.'

Petty Irritations

Sometimes the most trivial thing can set us off.
Like a tissue left in the pocket of our shorts
and the pulverised, fallout in the wash
is clinging relentlessly to everything else.
Or the battle to wrestle the childproof cap
from some medication, and the struggle over,
an explosion of tablets peppers the floor.

After joining the shortest supermarket queue,
the person in front has a price dispute
and as the duty manager is being summoned
you watch other checkout lines getting smaller.
Or your frustration when you are driving
and the car ahead slows up at an amber light
when you both had time to barrel through.

All this when no doubt, somewhere nearby,
circumstances over which we have no control
are changing ordinary lives like ours forever,
so despite a confidence in our own perspective,
I think that lurking inside most of us
there's an element of self-centred martyrdom
not likely to be admitted, even to ourselves.

A New Temptation

Would you believe,
a tattoo parlour has opened
in that vacant shop in town.
Tastefully fitted out
with nice curtains and furniture
it would give our hairdressers
a run for their money.

Through the window,
I can see several ladies perusing
glossy, illustrated brochures,
relaxed, smiling and chatting
on a comfortable lounge
while making their selection
of the one they want.

As a matter of fact,
it all looks so utterly inviting,
I'm tempted to get one myself.
Nah! Probably not.

An Idle Speculation

Summer is now blazing towards its seasonal demise,
the driest in decades so they say,
yet enervating humidity that never really morphed
into more than a trickle of rain
has been doggedly teasing us since the spring.
Most of the greenery is looking listless and wan
except the wisteria, rampaging on its usual assault.
The setting sun is remaining a burning ring of fire
as thankfully, it slips below the horizon
with a defiant, flashing glow of molten light,
ensuring we are in for another night of restlessness.

Yet the jacarandas had their best display in years,
the lavender-blue canopies arresting our attention.
The crepe myrtles lining the main street
and growing unpretentiously in almost every garden
have never been more eye-catchingly beautiful,
their pink bouquets still in breathtaking abundance
with no sign of any decline.
So despite all those climate change predictions,
I can't help wondering if a bored Mother Nature
is playing a cheeky game with we mortals
and the vagaries of her dominion making her laugh.

Simple Pleasures

On this early autumn Sunday morning,
our local park is already full of life.
The mist has lifted, sky clear azure blue
with just a hint of a pleasant cool breeze
making activity comfortable.

Eskies and rugs reserve tables and trees
in anticipation of picnic lunches.
Swings and roundabout are fully occupied,
slippery slide hosting small adventurers
as parents supervise and have a chat.
Embryo cyclists wobble along paths,
dogs chase balls with inexhaustible energy
and a superhero fights invisible villains
around the flower beds.

An elderly couple sit by the wisteria walk
observing this panorama of recreation,
the carefree view fuelling their smiles,
affirming that despite its inconsistencies,
we do live in a lucky country.

Decluttering

Having succumbed to the current fad,
I face my wardrobe with determination.
It is absolutely bursting at the seams
and all looks rather daunting
so I start on the shoe boxes underneath.
Half have been out of fashion for years
and not been worn for just as long
so virtuously, I throw them in the bin
for the charity shops won't want them.

Now in my stride, I check each hanger,
clothes forgotten and not worn for ever
as different fashions have taken over.
At the bedroom door the pile is growing,
but hang on a bit.
Maybe I should keep that black jacket
in case I need to go to a funeral
so I'd better retrieve the black shoes.
And might wear those sandals after all
with summer just around the corner.

In the end the wardrobe is almost as full
as it was before I started
and as I rehome the few empty hangers
know sentiment has had the last laugh
but vow next time to be utterly ruthless!

Choice

The election called,
it is anyone's guess
who will be victorious.
All over the country,
promises flow
from old campaigners
and young hopefuls,
a voracious media
reporting it all
to boring saturation.

By the actual day,
most of the citizens
will be so over it,
but it is what we pay
for the privilege of
a freedom to choose,
taking for granted
the civil right
that others overseas
are still fighting for.

Partners

In the supermarket aisle
the presence of a dog is surprising.
Despite its nondescript looks,
the smart coat and lead
exude a very privileged existence
and for a moment,
resent this woman's arrogance
for bringing her pet into the shop
instead of tying it up outside.

It is obviously not a guide dog
which I could understand
for its mistress is having no trouble
choosing her purchases.
However, animal lover that I am,
I stoop to fondle its ears
but thankfully, come up short
for on the coat is printed
'Please ignore me. I am working.'

The lady holding the lead
turns to me and smiles her thanks
for my prompt compliance
and I wonder about her disability
as her assistance companion
patiently observes,
its training focused and alert
to her current situation
as together, they both move on.

The Good Life

With winter just around the corner,
my old, tortoiseshell moggy Tess
has already begun her daily odyssey
to bask in the warmth of the sun.
With the usual savvy of an indoor cat,
she relocates around the windows
with timing accuracy,
as the provider of her comfort
continues on its journey to the west.

Bound by her personal routine
of nap time, lap time and meal time,
like most of our domestic felines
her life is always under her control,
the household merely there
to keep all the wheels turning,
and to reciprocate,
requiring only a judicious purr
when she deems it to be expedient.

Shopping

I can't seem to remember
to grab a carry bag
before walking through
a supermarket door
for just a couple of things.
Inevitably, the specials
will catch my eye
and some are so good
it makes sense to buy now
instead of full price later
and at the checkout,
need to purchase
yet another plastic bag
despite a car boot
now awash with them
from past misjudgements,
trusting that I am still
saving the environment.

Shifting Sands

On this diverse, multicultural planet of ours,
nations still have a few basics in common.
Everyone is getting older by the minute
regardless of their affluence or deprivation.
We share the sun, moon and stars,
tastebuds that appreciate something sweet,
same children's laughter in any language.
But while each region remains unique,
our own exists in a state of metamorphosis.

Transport and communication in transition,
medical breakthroughs offering hope,
other cultures introducing exotic cuisines.
Sufferers have issues instead of symptoms,
the local tip is a Waste Disposal Depot
and gaols upgraded to Correctional Facility
as new concepts continue to evolve,
but without the need to adapt to change,
whatever would be left to complain about?

Recognition

The shopping centre of our town
is showing its winter face,
the crepe myrtles not at their best,
OPEN signs displayed on doors
closed against the chill outside.
Woolly jacketed dogs accompany
rugged up shoppers
checking over the store windows
full of all things enticingly warm.

Workers are dashing back to jobs
with coffees and soups from cafes
offering hot winter specials
and with his usual, genuine smile,
the coatless seller of the *Big Issue*
is assuring concerned enquirers
that truly, he doesn't feel the cold.

But regardless of seasonal change,
there is a comfortable realisation
that at its fundamental core,
the town is remaining true to itself
in its predictable solidarity
and to our great good fortune,
we, are the current beneficiaries.

Possibilities?

A new sign now graces
a local business counter.
'Due to security issues,
we no longer accept cash
in payment for services.
Options are unchanged.'
Whatever next I wonder.
Guards at bank doors
frisking every customer
to forestall robberies?
Birth certificates carried
to prove identification?
Kids banned from pools?

Taking it even further.
Pubs and clubs closing
to save drunk gamblers
any self responsibility
or every mobile phone
monitored at all times
to detect terrorist plots?
When we can't use cash
for a basic transaction
then the inconceivable,
like horror of horrors,
pilotless passenger jets
could even eventuate!

Innocence

On the station platform, a pretty child
licks an ice cream and practices dance steps
while her mother gossips on the phone
and amused by her ingenuous behaviour,
he cannot help smiling
until the youngster, noticing his observation,
stops and points in his direction,
'What are ya lookin' at, ya horrible old perv,'
and though the arrival of his train
curtails the bystanders' hostile taunts,
the absolute injustice of their assumption
has really hurt his pride
and as distance assuages the humiliation,
he ruefully contemplates a reality
that not ALL angelic-looking kids are angels!

Jumping the Gun

With a few winter weeks left,
barren branches of maples
are etched against the sky.
Bare tangles of wisteria
are showing no trace of green
and dormant lawns slumber
without signs of any revival,
yet almost overnight,
wattles have sprung to life
in gold, gossamer profusion,
bouquets of azalea buds
are peeping through leaves
and a premature daffodil
is trembling in the breeze
so you can't help wondering
if winter, is treating us,
to a preview of the spring
while its chill is still lingering.

Mothercraft

Like a family of ducklings,
the preschoolers
in yellow vests and caps
file into the park.
For a while, they are halted
to observe a butterfly,
fluttering among the azaleas
but they are too impatient
to get to the swings
and it loses their interest.

In noisy high spirits,
they explore the delights
the playground offers
and after a reassuring count,
are led back for lunch
then settled down to nap,
allowing the mother ducks
to relax at last,
another safe excursion
tucked under their wings.

Misnomer

It appears that the traditional definition
of our libraries as a lender of books
may possibly become redundant.
Oh, the shelves of books are still there,
the librarians helpful at the front counter
but the man reading the local paper
and another perusing a fishing magazine
are now seated among multiple rows
of audio books, CDs and DVDs.

Students on laptops are sharing notes
absorbed in whispered conversations
and several of the computers are in use.
Notices of weekly board game sessions
and the upcoming 'Big Sale of Books'
share space with a pile of brochures
about lectures available on the internet.

But look. Over in the kids' corner,
a mother is reading to an attentive child
and another is making selections
with a preschooler showing interest,
so regardless of the council's efforts
to stay abreast of any new innovations,
perhaps for at least a little while yet,
no more shelves will be usurped
and books will continue to be relevant.

A Fresh Outlook

She believes that the best advice she was ever given
is to convert a half empty glass into one half full
to improve her well-being.
When the longed for rain was a disappointing drizzle
she was glad that at least, her garden and lawn
were being spared yet another day of drying out.
On a traffic island
in the middle of the highway's peak hour chaos,
changed her burgeoning impatience to relief
that she was already half way across.
So waiting at the doctor's surgery seeming endless,
she turns her fretting about lost working time
into a welcome break, selects a gossip magazine
and comfortably settles back to relax,
her wise old glass now turned in the right direction.

Gratification

One of the most satisfying feelings to have
must be getting into a bed
with freshly washed, sun-dried sheets.
Or maybe the first sip of morning coffee
soothing your brain back into gear
after a too late night.
Even waking up to a clear blue sky
on the day of your annual fund-raising fete
when the forecast had been uncertain.

Simply parking in the last available spot
at the local shops
with a 'to do' list as long as your arm
or lifting a perfectly risen birthday cake
from the oven to a cooling rack
on a very hectic, celebration morning
can really make a day,
ordinary moments gifting ordinary people
extraordinary pleasure.

Brainwaves

Around us
everywhere,
inspiration
can still be
hard to grasp
or blocked
out of reach,
but with luck,
a possibility
will invite us
to assess
its potential
or a spark
jog a memory.

Whether we
take a chance
or pass it by
is entirely
our decision
but the joy
of reviewing
a virgin idea
and nurturing
its journey
to conclusion
so fulfilling.

A Fruitful Thought

Preparing breakfast,
I pick up an orange
and start pondering
on its former history.
That years ago,
a tree was planted,
sustained to maturity
and progeny culled
to be relocated
for distribution
and ultimate display.

Much time and effort
went into this orange
before finding itself
in my kitchen
then into my hand,
yet in moments,
its reality will cease
for the brief pleasure
of a healthy start
to my daily routine.
Such is life I guess.

Feline Routine

In her privileged spot in front of the fire,
she sits bolt upright in the basket
preparing for her postprandial ablutions
before an afternoon nap.
After a thorough wash of her left paw,
she meticulously attends to her mouth,
her nose, those all-knowing ears,
her other paw completing the marathon.

There is no hint of absorption wavering,
as with long, languid strokes
her tongue institutes a thorough assault
on her stomach and nether regions
until content that the ritual is complete,
sniffs the bed to confirm that
nothing has defiled her personal domain
and after a brief circuit,
settles into the arms of Morpheus
to chase the cat next door in her dreams.

Azaleas

The early spring has my azalea hedge
fulfilling its stunning potential,
the solidarity of its roseate bouquets
a tribute to nature's engineering.
Dazzling enough to make me pause
every time I am passing by,
I remain in awe that such perfection
can flourish within my own domain.

As usual every year, I cannot resist
the desire to inhale its aroma
in case nature has refined its thinking,
even though I already know
there needs no further inducement
to capture my attention,
and a reaffirmed, lack of fragrance
can never debase its visual attraction.

While it slumbered through winter,
the hedge saw no acknowledgement
or concern about its well-being
yet once again, it is giving me its all
until much too soon
the herculean effort will take its toll
and jaded blooms carpet the grass,
my memory of its glory still blooming.

A Symptom of the Times

The trouble with Google
in regard to our health
is that too much information
in our inexperienced hands
can be quite unnerving.
With just a touch of a button
it can have us believing
we have the symptoms of
every affliction known to man.

So although it can contribute
some beneficial insight
for those in genuine need,
perhaps, for a lot of us,
these dalliances with the net
might be better served
by a strong cup of coffee
and power walk of the block
to maintain our equanimity.

Manoeuvres

A platoon of raucous cockatoos
is reconnoitring the back yard
but the early spring offerings
are leaner than they had envisaged.
The lemons are worth a nibble
but the mandarins are still in bud
and their annual prime objective,
the ancient peach tree,
now replaced with something else.

They gather around the birdbath
for a comfort stop and briefing
until a jubilant cry from their scout
further into the neighbourhood
has them screeching off
in an unmilitary disorder of wings
to plunder a more bountiful host,
the litter of wounded lemons
evidence of their aborted assault.

Just Raising a Point

G'day. I just want you to know that
it's no picnic being a crane.
All I ever do all day is lift and shift
other people's loads or stuff ups
that require all my strength
to stay firmly grounded
when a tricky load keeps swinging,
testing even Ted's experience.
It's just strain, strain, strain
and sometimes feel like giving up,
refuse to move anything
from here to there no matter what!

I'll admit, my life isn't always bad.
Ted's a savvy bloke, knows my limits
and most times he gets it right
but when he doesn't,
we are both deep in the proverbial,
and terribly embarrassed
to get a workmate in to help,
copping a mouthful from the boss
as well as the insurance assessor,
and take it from me,
it's simply no use being a crane
when your own spirits need lifting!

www.ingramcontent.com/pod-product-compliance
Lightning Source LLC
Chambersburg PA
CBHW062203100526
44589CB00014B/1932